BEMPATHY®

*Simplify Communication
by Looking at the Third Side
of the Coin*

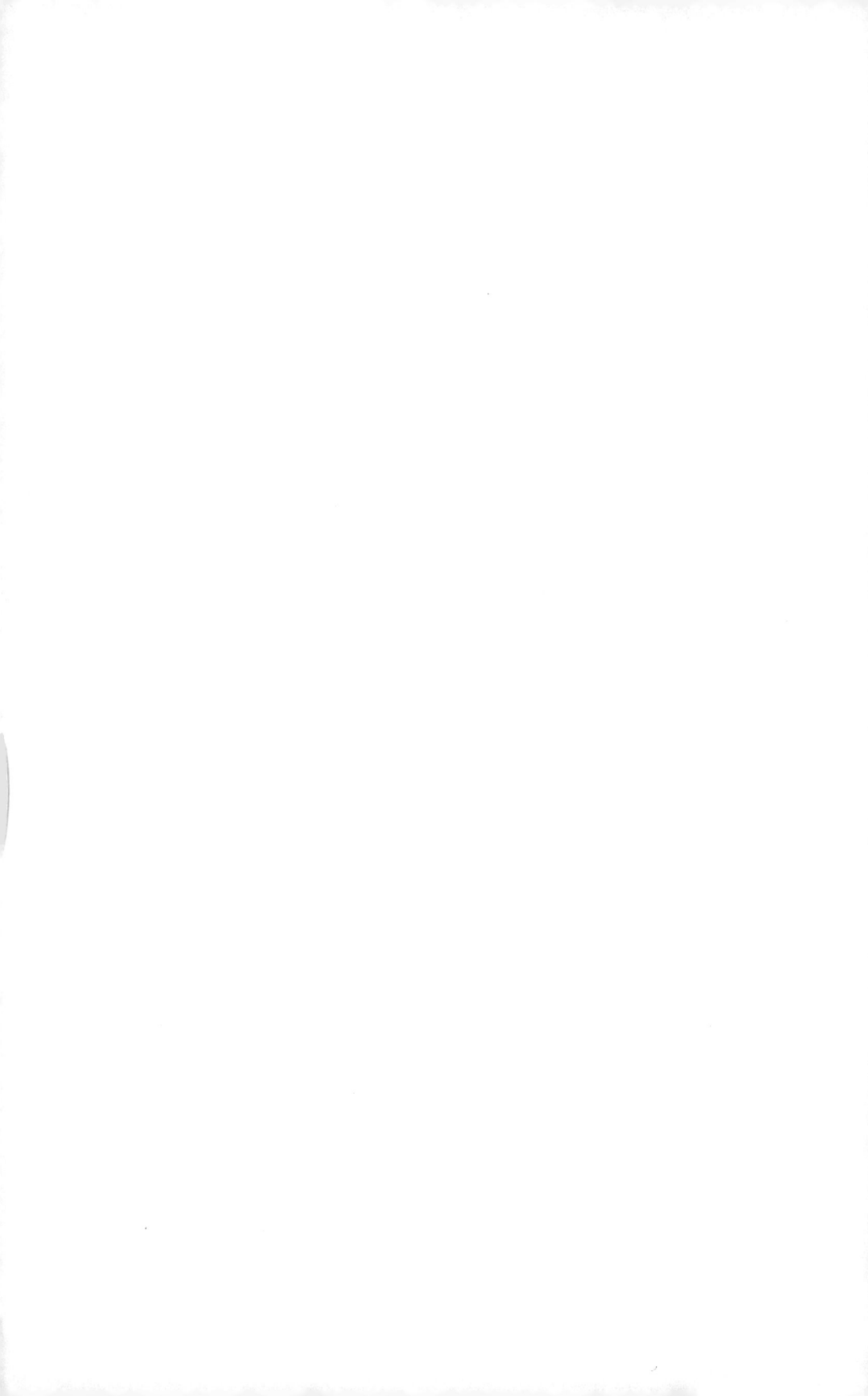

BEMPATHY®

*Simplify Communication
by Looking at the Third Side
of the Coin*

JILL ROBIN PAYNE
MA, LPC-S, LCDC

Edited by Taryn Lawson, Jessica Claire Haney and Ben Trittipoe
Cover Design by Jeremy Taylor
Interior Design by Cyndie Dahlberg
Character Illustrations by Jon Reis

Publishing and Media Inquiries:

6C Press
PO BOX 270563
Houston, TX 77277

ISBN: 978-1-961613-02-7 (paper book)
ISBN: 978-1-961613-03-4 (eBook)

Printed in the United States.

6CPress

Houston, TX
First Edition

DEDICATION

To my parents, Naomi and Bernard Zeavin; my son, Taylor; my brothers, Jerry, Spencer, and Brad. Most importantly, to my husband, Byron, for his patience and understanding.

CONTENTS

INTRODUCTION

Simplify your world using Bempathy, a process of bantering with empathy. The *Bempathy* series describes this revolutionary method of reciprocal communication, which can enhance social skills for people of all ages. This is the second book of the series, but the books can be read in any order, at any time, at any place!

There is a "new normal" since the COVID-19 pandemic, both positive and negative. Many adults are working from home, and some children are choosing to talk to their friends virtually instead of playing with them in person. Our lives are encased in many worlds: reality, virtual reality, augmented reality, metaverse, internet, and inner self.

This is a time when a new, positive way to communicate is needed to increase your productivity and decrease conflict, while improving your life and making it more optimistic. Transform the positives into something more positive and make the negatives work for you by converting your situations into win/win using an innovative new communicative technique called Bempathy. With easy-to-use skills, *Bempathy* gives short, sweet, timely, and important advice on connecting in a world of disconnectedness.

Interviews spanning over 30 years with more than 5,000 clients using Bempathy in counseling at pain clinics, behavioral hospitals, and private practice showed significant improvements in clients' relationships and emotional well-being, helping them achieve their goals. Feedback highlighted various benefits, including understanding their priorities and values, finding suitable partners, setting boundaries, avoiding mistakes, and managing emotions. Clients found the process enjoyable, with a positive impact on their lives. Bempathy fostered better self-understanding, supportive coaching, a sense of care, clarity in personal issues, and enhanced relationship awareness. The approach led to sustainable, healthy partnerships and encouraged positive affirmations. Counseling was gentle, patient, empathetic, and nudged clients towards accountability. (This is qualitative research).

Bempathy has three full-of-life cartoon characters that will grab your attention and take you through an entertaining fictional story, while relating vital information for better communication. The complex analytical communication techniques are simplified as the characters illustrate how to brighten up dim situations. Learn how to see another's perspective and move forward in your life by increasing your comfortability while overcoming conflicts. In a society that is creating an "all or nothing" culture, it is crucial that people realize there is a third side to the coin—the side that is small with ridges and is difficult to see.

Follow *Bempathy's* three charming characters—Beacon, Brighten, and Bow— as they dive deeper into new, effective approaches, such as the *Map of Reflection, Dynamic Watchfulness, Conversing with Self,* and more.

Enjoy the read!

CHAPTER 1
The Need for Bempathy

Welcome to a "lit" life using Bempathy, which is banter with empathy. This is an innovative reciprocal communication style with easy-to-use skills that can help transform your life into many successful situations. The COVID-19 pandemic left us with a "new normal" that has pros and cons. Many people want to work from home virtually, some children now prefer to stay in their rooms and chat with their friends online instead of physically playing with them. Some people prefer a text over a phone call after meeting, believing it is rude to call first. This is a perfect time to introduce this new and better way to communicate, increasing connectedness with others, and making situations work for you.

Bempathy is an interpersonal technique of verbal and nonverbal communication that facilitates congruent conversation between people. This book will improve your life and increase productivity. Bempathy has six key elements, the 6 C's: communication, commonality, connectedness, comfortability, control, and commitment.

The three engaging cartoon characters lead you on a fictional journey, while equipping you with tools for overcoming conflict. They take you down memory lane, back to when most things in life were simpler and more fun. Each character represents a different personality type, with varying moods and mindsets with which people of all ages can identify, while recognizing how self-identity influences perceptions and experiences.

Beacon, Brighten, and Bow illustrate the three personality types: a leader, a follower, and a compromiser. The fraternal twins are Beacon, who leads the way, and Brighten, who follows and is enlightened. Bow the dog helps connect the dots. These characters take difficult analytical techniques in the communication process and simplify them by looking through children's eyes.

This amusing journey down Bempathy lane is the second *Bempathy* book of a series that promotes discussion and getting along by creating satisfying social situations, versus ghosting or canceling. Sometimes we need to step back emotionally, behaviorally, or both to be able to see a different perspective. Ghosting is when someone in your life ends the relationship abruptly with no explanation, whether they're a friend, family member, or lover—becoming a "ghost" by disappearing. Canceling, on the other hand, is usually when a public figure or company is shunned on Twitter or other social media platforms. Therefore, they become an outcast, and anything they do brings backlash. The "all or nothing" thinking and behavior may be creating an "all or nothing" society. *I'm right, you're wrong, therefore I'm blocking you out of my life, the world, everything!* We need to remember that nobody is perfect, including ourselves, and that there is something called a Freudian slip, or foot in the mouth.

What happened to another perspective, the in-between, and seeing the third side of the coin? Seeing another perspective is sometimes difficult; however, it is necessary for resolution and compromise.

The dynamics of "all or nothing" thinking may leave some people with what is called "unfinished business." In psychology, this can lead to negative feelings and behaviors, such as depression, irritation, anger, anxiety, social anxiety, excessive stress, and acting out. Some examples of acting out in our society are an increase in drug and alcohol abuse, physical or verbal fighting, throwing fits, stealing, and reckless behavior, such as an increase in car fatalities and crime in the past few years. Acting out is a negative way to release stress, which tends to push people away and cause disconnection. Bempathy, on the other hand, gets people to connect, finding common ground and commonality.

People have a need to feel complete and be heard. That is one reason cultures have rituals when starting or ending something. Funerals, weddings, and graduations are just some of the rituals that help us move from one stage of life to another. In our society, because of unfinished business, some people may be holding on to residual feelings. These rituals help us move forward and feel unstuck.

People are motivated to survive. Therefore, when someone perceives themselves as being threatened, even if they are not, they go into survival mode. This causes them to focus only on themselves, blinding them to the big picture, which may be causing societal issues.

The information below inspired Beacon, Brighten, and Bow to work together to tell their story:

*87% **of Americans are stressed:** American Psychological Association's (APA) recent poll states stress continues to be on the rise since the COVID-19 pandemic (2021, 2022). Some symptoms are depression, anxiety, anger, irritability, feeling* *overwhelmed, poor memory, social anxiety, and lack of motivation, which are* **mental health issues.**

Confirmation bias: *People tend to pick information that supports their view while remaining blinded to or ignoring opposing information. Most of us do this in some form or another, causing people to have all-or-nothing thinking if never opposed. Confirmation bias is reinforced by the internet's "Filter Bubble," which continues to send us information using algorithms to validate our beliefs. It's important for us to ask ourselves questions, such as who is creating the algorithms, and how are they created? Who benefits from them? People are blinded from seeing other perspectives, resulting in something called the "Backfire Effect," which may push people to lean further into their biased belief, causing increased emotions. (Chamorro-Premuzic, 2014; Suzuki & Yamamoto, 2021)*

Some preventatives for confirmation bias are below.
1. Do not argue or try to prove you are right.
2. Cognitively empathize with others.
3. Keep emotions out of it.
4. Discuss, don't attack.
5. Listen and respect facts; you don't need to agree.
6. Repeat what the other person said in your own words to make sure you heard them correctly.
7. Sometimes allow the other person to have the last word.

Benjamin Franklin Effect: *This is a psychological phenomenon that boosts loyalty, even when the relationship is not strong. If you dislike a person, but they get you to do something simple for them—something you do automatically, like opening a door—you're then going to experience cognitive dissonance. It will feel uncomfortable to help a person who you don't like. In order to resolve this dissonance, you need to match your mindset to your actions. Thus, you are more likely to repeat the favor or other positive behaviors toward this person, especially if the person shows appreciation. (McRaney, 2011; Seyfried, 2022)*

Broken Heart Syndrome: *Yes, you can die of a broken heart; however, it is also extremely unlikely. Stressful situations or extreme emotions, such as the loss of loved ones or a job, moving, having surgery, etc. can be life-threatening (Healthwise Staff, 2021). These stressful events trigger a surge of stress hormones, which can put you in short-term heart failure (Cleveland Clinic, 2020).*

Emotional Contagion: Both positive and negative emotions, like happiness or anger, can be transferred to others, leading people to "catch" the emotions of others. They will spread like a virus. Research has shown that social media is one major source of the spread. (Kramer et al., 2014).

Let's turn the pages and bring back some of our happier childhood memories, returning to a time when we found pleasure and excitement in the little things in life. Delight in empathizing and relating with these cool characters.

Start by asking yourself, how do you feel at this moment in time? Then circle the face that best represents your feeling on the next page. After you do that, identify each character's emotion, then match them with the other character with the same emotion. Simply place the number of the emotion above the character's face that exhibits that emotion, then match it with the other character. The numbers to the emotions are seen below:

1 — Anger
2 — Disgust
3 — Fear
4 — Happiness
5 — Sadness
6 — Surprise

The answers are found in Chapter 6 on page 64.

This activity is a fun way to improve your concentration, memory, thinking skills, and relaxation, as well as facilitate empathy. It will increase your awareness of different emotions in different people and yourself.

Let's use this new knowledge to improve our present life.
As you turn the pages, work to leave the
negative memories in the past.

CHAPTER 2
Welcome to a Brighter Life

Beacon asked his sister, "Could our societal norms, along with constantly being inundated with information, be promoting negative behavior? Generating conflict? Anxiety? Anger? Mental illness? How can we learn from our mistakes if we are not given a chance to explain, change, or look at another perspective? Could all the different worlds we inhabit—such as physical, digital, and biological—be confusing and overwhelming us? There is something called epigenetics, the study of how our behavior and environment affect the way our genes work. These gene modifications can be both negative and positive."

Feeling overwhelmed by all these ideas, Beacon, Brighten, and Bow grimaced. They contemplated how to work with our new worlds—reality, virtual reality, augmented reality, metaverse, internet, and our inner self—to make a more harmonious life where we can be heard, accepted, appreciated, and get our needs met. They all discussed the importance of spreading the word about how to use the six key elements of Bempathy, the 6 C's, to make situations prosperous.

Beacon reminded Brighten and Bow of the definitions of the six key elements:

1. Communication — The ability to send and receive information that another person will understand; the ability to send and receive information to oneself.
2. Commonality — Two or more people who share the same or similar characteristics, interests, or experiences on such subjects as people, places, or things.
3. Connectedness — A feeling of fitting in or being linked with self or one or more people.
4. Comfortability — The ability to feel comfortable in a situation and/or with self; feeling physically and/or emotionally at ease; freedom from emotional or physical pain.
5. Control — The ability to perceive power, exercise limits, or have a guiding influence over situations and self.
6. Commitment — The state of being dedicated or loyal to self, something, or someone.

Beacon, Brighten, and Bow realized that if a person wants to be able to communicate and connect with others, they first need to communicate and connect with themselves. People's minds and emotions need to match their behavior so that they feel connected with themselves, and therefore comfortable with themselves. When people are comfortable in their own skin, they feel comfortable with others and in different situations. Beacon calls this *Cognitive Behavioral Emotional Congruence.*

The first *Bempathy* book discussed the importance of the six key elements. All of these can produce congruent conversation; however, using one or two, or any combination thereof, can create even more successful communication. To create an outcome we want, our inner self needs to match our behavior.

When we are not communicating congruently within ourselves, we are creating a disconnect. How can we communicate with others if we can't communicate with ourselves? Incongruence causes us to have discomfort, resulting in negative feelings and negative communication with others in our world.

Beacon likes to give examples when explaining these concepts, which helps Brighten and Bow visualize what he is saying. He explained that we are the center of our world. When we are mad, our world is mad. When we are sad, our world is sad. When we are happy, so is our world. Action creates reaction.

Our thoughts, emotions, and behaviors need to *communicate commonality* in order for us to feel *connected* and *comfortable* with ourselves. This gives us a feeling of *control* so we can *commit* to moving forward. Also, knowing where to place the people, places, and things in our lives will give us a sense of control, decrease fear and anxiety, and motivate us to step forward and reach our dreams.

Beacon loves to create different methods to improve the lives of Brighten, Bow, and others. He calls these methods "games" or "activities" because it puts a fun spin on them. If you are an adult, the word *game* may take you back to fun memories of when you were younger. If you are youthful, games make you think of playing, which is just plain fun. Beacon knows words are extremely important and have different connotations. *Games* are associated with fun, and *methods* are associated with work. Beacon created the Map of Reflection, Dynamic Watchfulness, and Conversing with Self,

which are some of the games he wants to explain to you, Brighten, and Bow in the next chapters.

Beacon asked, "Are we getting into an electronic *cage* in an electronic *age*?" He proposed, "Mindfulness is not enough anymore, since we now have virtual reality...possibly electronic implants in the future."

Humans themselves are also integrating with technology, as evidenced by neural implants that change how our brains work. This is another new world that science is exploring where we also need Dynamic Watchfulness. We must be on high alert and watchful of what is real and what is not. These new technologies have upsides and downsides. The positives are, we may live longer and healthier, but what are we giving up? Currently, it is unknown. People need to step back and see the whole picture.

Ponce de Leon looked for the Fountain of Youth; is this it? Being half-human and half-technology? We don't know yet. You have heard of the bionic man. We are there.

What if dementia can be eradicated with one small brain implant? Would you do it? Dr. Kevin Warwick, known as Captain Cyborg, a professor of cybernetics at Reading University, is experimenting with creating cyborgs using electronic implants.

Dr. Warwick may eventually have the answers to these questions. If the implants are put in a robot, the robots could become globally connected, like the internet. There is fear that military robots in the network may learn to think independently, as foreshadowed by the 1984 movie *The Terminator*. Dr. Warwick says there are dangers to think about, yet he also believes these experiments will advance science. We'll need to pay attention to these issues as they develop, but our brains already have a lot to grapple with.

Beacon deliberated, "Research shows being immersed in virtual reality can confuse the brain about what is real and what is not. We need to be dynamic in our watchfulness so that we stay in control and feel safe. With constantly changing *dynamics*, we need to be *watchful* of how the changes affect us and how we affect the changes.

"For example, emotions can overflow from one person to another, and can also flow from the internet to people. They can be contagious, just like a smile.

Therefore, in a world overflowing with technology, empathy is best expressed by banter and Dynamic Watchfulness. This will promote a more synchronized life to help guide us through the overflow. These strategies help us work with technology to find a balance."

Dynamic Watchfulness is defined as:

1. The state of being active and present in the multiple worlds—reality, virtual reality, metaverse, internet, inner self, and others that are constantly evolving—that constitute our lives, and understanding the difference between them.
2. The quality or state of being aware of and attentive to the consequences of actions in the context of multiple information sources, such as reality, virtual reality, metaverse, internet, inner self, and cybernetics.
3. Continuous observation of oneself, electronic devices, and others; understanding what is done or occurs; practicing caution, discretion, and self-restraint; being vigilantly on guard and alert to signs; watchfully anticipating and maintaining respect for all worlds.
4. The use of the five senses, as well as help from others, to be dynamic in our watchfulness of all the worlds in which we live.

Our brain is too easily fooled. Illusions, algorithms, and information overload are confusing and overwhelming for the human brain, creating humans who make poor choices, or no choices at all. Dynamic Watchfulness is adding Bempathizing to mindfulness. Banter with empathy. To connect with a person, we must empathetically banter with them. This is important in building a trusting relationship.

It is essential to have an accomplice in this world to help us differentiate what is real, what is not, and what works for us. Two heads are better than one. The accomplice can be a friend, colleague, family member, doctor, lawyer, therapist, teacher, etc. Think of an accomplice as someone who you can collaborate with and who assists you, in a trusting atmosphere, to see the third side of the coin, a new perspective. Beacon, Brighten, and Bow are perfect examples of what accomplices are and how they act. Following them through this book will reiterate what an accomplice is.

Social media, virtual reality, metaverse, and information overload can be disruptive, causing disconnect instead of connection. Being dynamically watchful will allow us to monitor these things—how they affect us, and how we affect them. It is a reciprocal relationship.

Technology is advancing rapidly. It is difficult for humans to keep up with the many directions in which it is going. Therefore, we need to be dynamic in our response to these quickly changing times. We need to be watchful, alert, and vigilant to overpower what could otherwise be confusing or overwhelming.

Dynamic Watchfulness Questions to Ask Yourself

What behaviors and ways of thinking are overflowing into your world?
Are you in reality, or in the virtual world?
How dependent are you on electronic devices?

How do you feel when you are on the internet?
How is your world on the internet?
       Happy, sad, anxiety-producing?
       What are the words you use?
       Do you use the same words when you meet face to face?
Is the pace the same on the internet as it is in the real world?

How is social media affecting your face-to-face interactions?
Is it affecting your behavior?
When does it affect your behavior?

How are your limits on the internet versus face to face?
       Do they work for you on the internet?
       Do they work for you face to face?
How much space is between people on the internet versus face to face?
Is the pace working for you? Is this person real, a hologram, or a cyborg?

What are the limits on the internet? Endless?
What are your limits on the internet? Endless?
What are your limits in the real world? Limited?

How is the internet thinking?
How is the internet behaving?

What emotions are the internet expressing? Think of emotional contagion, which was explained in Chapter One.

People are inundated with electronics, never-ending text messages, never-ending news, never-ending...
This is a good time to discuss the above questions with your accomplice. By bantering back and forth and empathizing with your accomplice, you will be able to come up with healthy answers to help you move forward from point A to point B. Where is the here and now on the internet or in virtual reality? Dynamic Watchfulness will help us maneuver in these new worlds by asking the questions above. Beacon, Brighten, and Bow will show you some activities from Dynamic Watchfulness to help you.

Brighten jumped up and down with Bow in excitement, saying, "I can't wait to play these games and enlighten my friends along the way to become comfortable with themselves and others, promoting healthier and happier outcomes for their future."

Have fun learning new communication skills from Beacon, Brighten, and Bow as they use Bempathy to handle their conflicts and dilemmas.

CHAPTER 3
Beacon Illuminates a New Bempathy Concept: Conversing with Self

Beacon has been a leader ever since he was born, popping out a minute before his fraternal twin Brighten, and leading the way into a bright new world. He is the guiding light that continues to enlighten his sister, their dog, and others in a constantly changing environment. Brighten follows Beacon and looks up to him—what he says and does. Bow, their dog, stands by her side to comfort her and make sense of Beacon's innovative games and activities.

Beacon continually talks about the importance of Bempathizing with others to help make situations successful. He reminds Brighten and Bow what Bempathizers are:

> Bempathizers are sincere. They recognize how to build camaraderie by listening and being patient while working at cognitively empathizing to see different perspectives. They engage in banter/chit-chat with an awareness of TP (timing and position). They know when and where to bring up certain topics and when to step back emotionally, physically, or both, to see another side. They know how to make conversations flow reciprocally, increasing congruency in the subject matter by using Dynamic Watchfulness along with the six key elements, the 6 C's: communication, commonality, connectedness, comfortability, control, and commitment. These elements help to create balance and compromise. Not only are Bempathizers aware that action creates reaction and vice versa, they realize that life is perception, and perception is life.

Beacon is aware that even though everything is relational and situational, we still need to remember that everyone is different and has a different language depending on their history, genetics, and environments. The basics are the same—people want to feel heard, appreciated, and accepted.

Sometimes, when Beacon is feeling out-of-sorts, he utilizes a game he calls Conversing with Self. This is one of the maneuvers for Dynamic Watchfulness—helping us to be more aware of our different worlds and the importance of understanding and getting along with them. This game helps him think clearer in his inner world and eventually feel more comfortable. Bantering and empathizing with yourself creates connectedness, stimulating unconditional love.

At first, when Beacon does this game, he says it feels weird because he is not used to talking out loud to himself and answering back. This is considered out of the norm. Therefore, he makes sure that when he does this game, no one's around and it is extremely private. Beacon understands that talking out loud when other people are around is also an invasion of their personal space.

One day, Beacon explained to Brighten, "First, let's learn to communicate out loud with ourselves, finding commonality within ourselves so we feel more connected and can relate better with others. Using some or all of the six key elements on ourselves helps us feel more comfortable, encouraging our thoughts to match our feelings and behavior, finding commonality. This increases our ability to connect with ourselves, which, in turn, increases our comfortability and makes us feel more in control, in order to move forward."

Brighten laughed and said, "Talking to yourself? Isn't that weird?"

Beacon chuckled, "Yes, it feels that way at first. Many people talk to themselves every now and then. Haven't you heard me mumble to myself when I get frustrated? It helps me to focus! There are even studies showing that if you talk out loud to yourself in the third person, this can help you regulate your emotions and put things in perspective."

Brighten smiled. "Sounds interesting," she said. "Does it work for you?"

Beacon pondered for a moment, then said, "It does when I do it the Bempathy way, which is going a step further and actually conversing with myself out loud in the third person, then answering myself out loud in the third person. It's conversational, using open-ended questions to myself! It's as though you are talking to another person. Sometimes I even write down what I learned to help me make sense of things. It's best to do this in private."

Brighten giggled. "Yeah, right!" she exclaimed.

Bow barked in agreement, thinking, "We need to stop, look at, and listen to ourselves and get connected with our thoughts, feelings, and behaviors before we can do it with others!"

Beacon recounted: "The more congruent our inner voice is, the more connected and comfortable we become with ourselves. The more connected and comfortable we are with ourselves, the more motivated we are to be face to face with others. This is the first step to getting our wants and needs met with others. When our thoughts conflict with our emotions or behavior, or both, we are creating disconnect, discomfort, and anxiety. When our inner thoughts coincide with matching emotions and behavior, we create an outcome that we most likely want."

In the first *Bempathy* book, we talked about how when our thoughts are in our head, it's difficult sometimes to make sense of them. The thoughts tend to run together and race. When you take them out of your head and speak, you can actually hear what you are saying and answering. It interrupts the thought process and slows it down. Studies show the more senses you use, the more you can make sense of things. Also, talking aloud to yourself in the third person increases self-control, improving decision-making.

Then Beacon explained the purpose of Conversing with Self to help motivate Brighten to:

- Get a clear vision.
- Rationalize things.
- Take herself out of the situation.
- Look at the bigger picture.
- Put things in perspective.
- Give another perspective.
- Stop and think.
- Slow down thoughts.
- Prioritize.
- Diffuse the situation and improve focus.

After Beacon spoke about the importance of connecting with yourself to Brighten, he explained how to do the Conversing with Self game:

1. Do this when feeling uncomfortable with yourself.
2. Pick a private spot.
3. Use suggested questions ("Who...? What...? Where...? How...?").
4. Answer with more than one word. Elaborate.
5. Avoid using "you" or "why," because starting a sentence with these words puts people on the defensive.
6. Resist using the word *but*, which takes power away from the preceded statements.
7. Instead of saying "I" or "me," talk in the third person, using your name. This distances you from the conversation.
8. Be inquisitive, not critical.
9. Be conversational; don't interrogate.
10. *Optional:* When realizing what you want, write it down and define it so you can read it.

Brighten was excited to experience this game as soon as possible to help her get out of her rut. Bow wagged her tail in agreement. Brighten immediately went to a private place in the house where no one could hear her and started conversing aloud with herself in the third person. Below is an example of Brighten doing the Conversing with Self game.

Q: How are Brighten's actions matching her values?
A: Honestly, not sure. She rationalizes her behavior by thinking staying in her room is good for her and she doesn't need to see people in person because she can do anything on the internet. She knows that being alone in her room constantly isn't healthy for her and she gets sad. She is afraid of what will happen if she goes out in the neighborhood. She knows that this doesn't make sense. **Brighten's thoughts don't match her behavior.**

Q: What benefits does Brighten gain from this behavior? What's in it for her?
A: It's easy, comfortable, and safe!

Q: What is the worst thing that would happen to Brighten if she walked around her neighborhood?
A: Nothing. She may meet someone, but she wouldn't know what to say.

Q: What are things Brighten says to family members?

A: She talks about her gaming and asks about how they feel. She guesses she could just ask people things about themselves and let them do most of the talking. Every morning she could say affirmations about how fun she is and take baby steps to be with more positive people.

Q: What does Brighten think about this answer?
A: She feels content at this time.

Below are the prompts and questions that Brighten asked herself before playing the game.

My thoughts are...
My behavior is...
My dynamics or environment are...
My outcome is...
What outcome do I want?
Is this the outcome I want? Yes or no

Her answer was no, which told her that her thoughts and behavior weren't matching and that it was a great time to do the Conversing with Self game. Ask yourself the questions above to see if today would be a good time to play the same game.

Was your answer about the outcome you wanted yes, or no? Remember being congruent or incongruent with yourself is going to affect how you relate with others and vice versa.

Let's turn back time, to childhood memories of when things were simpler.
Enjoy Beacon, Brighten, and Bow's story of overcoming conflicts and dilemmas the
Bempathy way.

CHAPTER 4
Handling Dilemmas and Conflicts

Beacon, Brighten, and Bow moved from their medium-sized house and medium-sized neighborhood to a bigger, brighter house and neighborhood. Even though Brighten was excited and happy about her new move to a better place, she also felt a loss and a fear of missing out, FOMO.

Leaving all her friends and her old neighborhood frightened Brighten. She had bouts of loneliness and a feeling of disconnection. She tended to stay in her room and engaged only digitally with her friends. Sometimes her friends were slow to respond, causing her to get upset and anxious. Bow sensed this and nuzzled up to her often to try to decrease her anxiety and sadness.

Beacon, on the other hand, enjoys new environments, finding them exciting. He keeps up with his friends by texting or calling them to get together and do fun things. As Beacon, Brighten, and Bow were unpacking all their belongings, Brighten began ruminating and she started to cry. Bow, her faithful dog who helped her make sense of things, stayed by her side, snuggling up to her for a hug. Brighten loved having Bow around for comfort because Bow always understood her.

Beacon looked perplexed and said, "Brighten, what's wrong?"

Brighten was saddened and said, "I'm upset about my old friends forgetting me, and afraid that no one in the new neighborhood will like me."

Beacon reflected on what Brighten said. He then consoled his sister with one of the many analogies he liked to use when problems arose. "Think of life as mathematical equations," he said. "Let's do a math lesson!"

Brighten sighed and slumped simultaneously in exasperation because she didn't like math.

Beacon quickly went to his whiteboard, which they keep accessible because they know writing things down helps people make sense of things, keep track, and feel more in control. Beacon said, "Let's look at pluses and

minuses. Brighten, if I gave you $100 and added $100 more, what would you get?"

She laughed, "That's easy, $200!"

Beacon smiled and proceeded to do more. "Now let's change that sign to a minus. What is the total now?"

Brighten frowned and said, "A big fat zero."

Beacon suggested, "That's what happens in life when we have too many negatives. If you keep subtracting throughout the day with negative thoughts and/or actions, you will have a big fat zero at the end of the day. There are only twenty-four hours in the day, so replace the negatives with positives or turn the negatives into positives, making life run smoother."

He suggested, "How about we try the Map of Reflection game? This will help you put things in perspective, prioritize what is beneficial in your life, and remove unwanted negatives. So, when doing your Map of Reflection, you need to ask yourself if the things in your life are adding or subtracting. Then choose where you want to place them in relation to yourself in the center. You are the most important person in your world; therefore, you are located in the center of your Map of Reflection and all the people, places, and things in your life surround you."

Bow wagged her tail in excitement, barking at this new, groundbreaking way to gain more control over their lives.

Brighten looked confused and said, "I don't want to be self-centered!"

Beacon laughed. "This doesn't mean you are self-centered. You are the center of *your* world, not the center of *the* world. When we put ourselves first, that means we are conscious of ourselves and how our feelings and behavior affect our world and vice versa. You are giving yourself unconditional love. Our time and attention are limited, which makes every minute valuable. Since we don't have control over our forever-changing world, what do we have control over?"

Brighten shouted, "Our time and attention and what we do with it!"

Map of Reflection

Bow howled, jumping up and down in excitement.

Beacon smiled as he drew a picture of the Map of Reflection. He began lecturing, as he liked to do. "Making a list of the people, places, and things in your life, then placing them in the specific rings will organize your desires, needs, and wants. You can visually see your placements. Pay close attention to those things you might think are necessary, but, *upon reflection*, can be released into the 'Spring Cleaning' section. Just because something is in Spring Cleaning doesn't mean that it can't fluctuate back into a closer part of your life later. This might include old friends; old feelings, like resentment; or places, like work and school."

Beacon went on. "Think of your Map of Reflection as your world displayed flat, and you are in the center reacting to your world as your world reacts to you. The blue section is the water around, it ebbs and flows. The things in that area are floating, and they may fall off your world or swim back into your life when and if *you* decide. This is your reflection of your present world."

Stepping away from the board, Beacon said, "Consider all areas of your life: family, faith/spiritual, social, occupation, leisure activities, psychological and emotional distractions, personal development, and vanity-related priorities. Be honest with yourself. This is your Map of Reflection in a snapshot of time, open to change as often as necessary. After you complete your Map of Reflection, sometimes doing the Conversing with Self, it will help clarify your reflection even more. All of this is a part of Dynamic Watchfulness."

Brighten then made a list of three categories—persons, places, and things—and wrote down everything in her life. She placed the information into the different rings in the drawing of her Map of Reflection. She prioritized without thinking of boundaries because boundaries get too complicated. Boundaries put limits on a person's life, which is why the Map of Reflection works better. It regulates your intimate relationships between people, places, and things.

Brighten shared her insights after doing the Map of Reflection game. She exclaimed, "Wow, after visually reflecting, I can see old friends are still in my life, and new friends are on the horizon. This game got me to ask myself, 'How come I allow persons, places, and things to control my

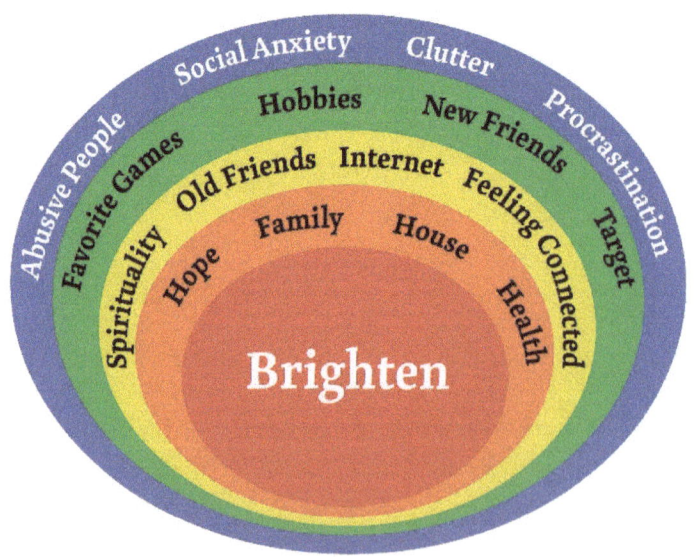

mood, thoughts, and behavior? Am I really upset with someone or something else, or actually upset with myself?' I am the center of my world; therefore, I can choose how I respond. Everything I do or is done to me is 'noise,' like the static on the phone or glitches when Zooming. This frustrates me, causing things to be harder to see and understand. This map helps me filter out some of my noise so I can hear myself think and hear others more clearly."

Just as Brighten finished her statement, Bow saw a squirrel and chased it, barking all the way to their neighbor's house. Brighten ran after her, bumping into a new young neighbor who stopped Bow by grabbing her collar. Brighten felt awkward and embarrassed about Bow not being on a leash. She didn't know what to say except "thank you" and ran back home with Bow.

Brighten bowed her head. "Beacon, I just don't know what to do with myself," she said. "The only place I feel comfortable and safe is in my room! My mind tells me to go out and have fun with our neighbors, but my anxiety tells me 'NO' which stops me. I'm just not motivated."

Bow nudged Brighten toward the door, barking, wanting her to go visit the neighbor.

Brighten shook her head in frustration over how her thoughts didn't match her behavior and sighed. She felt conflicted. Just then, she had an epiphany.

This is a great time to say my affirmations, Brighten thought. *When I did the game Conversing with Self, I found out saying affirmations are baby steps toward reaching my goals. What affirmations should I think and say?* She continued in deep thought. *I know!*

Just then, Brighten started to repeat a realistic affirmation. She knew she liked some people, and some people liked her, so she dropped the word "some" and said, "I like people and people like me!" Brighten immediately started to smile.

Beacon asked her, "What are you thinking?"

She smiled and said, "Positive thoughts! Let's put our heads together to come up with a solution about our friend situation!"

The trio sat together thinking about what to do about their friends. They thought and thought and thought about what to do with this dilemma. Conversing back and forth, trying to come up with a solution, led to them all getting headaches. They decided to take a break from the issue and relax by playing fetch with Bow.

Bow was having so much fun fetching. She was on a roll. She saw the mail carrier and started to chase them down the street.

Beacon and Brighten immediately ran after her, screaming all the way, "STOP!"

It's a good thing that Bow loves everyone and can see all different perspectives. She happily wagged her tail and opened her mouth so the mail carrier could put the mail there. Bow, being a compromiser, decided that the pile of mail needed to be distributed fairly, and dropped it on the floor for all to share and sort by name.

Beacon and Brighten saw letters with their names on them and opened them up. To Brighten's surprise, she had received an invitation from her old friends, requesting that both she and her brother come to a birthday party! The invitation also asked them to sing duets, which is what they usually did at parties. They were known for their fabulous voices and creating witty songs. Together they said, "Wow, this is fantastic!" They all jumped up and down with joy and excitement.

As Brighten opened a second letter, her facial expression went from happy to befuddlement. Beacon asked, "What's wrong, Brighten? You look troubled."

Brighten frowned. "We have a dilemma," she said. "We are both invited to two important parties at once: one with our old friends, and one with our new ones. Now I have a chance to meet new friends at this block party, but I also want to keep in touch with my old friends. I don't know what to do!"

Beacon looked at the invitation from their old friends and smiled. He said, "Brighten, what our old friends really want is for us to sing our duets and be the entertainment for the party. I understand you don't want to disappoint your friends and you would like to go to both events, but you physically cannot."

Brighten frowned and said, "You're right, as usual."

Beacon pondered briefly and said, "Let's step back and think of some possibilities. When we did our duets in front of our friends, how did they respond?"

Brighten's eyes widened. "They roared for more and some of them actually recorded what we sang on their phones," she said.

Beacon asked, "Do you think all our old friends will bring their phones to the party?"

Brighten laughed and said, "They don't leave their homes without them."

Beacon held up a finger, which was a common habit when he thought an idea had merit. "What would you say to making a holographic display of us singing duets and then sending them to our old friends?" he asked.

Brighten chuckled and responded, "Fantabulous! You saved the day! Now I won't feel guilty about going to the block party to meet new friends the same day." All three jumped up and down, laughing in unison.

Brighten and Bow's faces beamed. Bow cocked her head, gave a canine smile, and wagged her tail at the thought of doing this. Beacon suggested, "All we need is some reasonable equipment, hologram film, virtual reality glasses, and a projector to do a 3D scan of us singing together. Then we just animate the scan. What a fun project!"

Brighten giggled and said, "Wow, what an enlightening idea, Beacon! We will be 'unreal'—bigger than life! Our friends love holograms and virtual reality because it is exciting and entertaining. This will get them to associate us with being fun and amazing!"

All three got together to plan how they would accomplish this feat. They spent hours researching on the internet, talking, and writing down what to do for their hologram presentation. Each one was given different duties. Beacon was in charge of working with the laser, cutting, and setting up for the 3D hologram. Brighten was in charge of working with the animation portion and Bow, as usual, was there to oversee everything and make sure it was done right.

As they progressed, they talked about the importance of using Dynamic Watchfulness as they created a hologram that was a "fake" version of themselves. They asked each other how this would affect their relationships. They agreed it would be both positive and negative. The positive is that this was fun and both sides will win. The negative is that we have one brain and so far, we cannot be split in half to experience being in two places at once. So, we will miss the fun that our friends experience watching us. This is a part of being dynamic in their watchfulness.

Beacon commented how wonderful it was to have trusting individuals in his life, like Brighten and Bow. "Making one true friend in the real world can help give us another perspective," he said. "This is a large part of what distinguishes Dynamic Watchfulness from mindfulness."

Brighten and Bow smiled in agreement as they looked forward to finishing their project.

Beacon and Brighten realized that when our brain is immersed in virtual reality, it gets confused, thinking it is real. Having another person to help us practice caution by being vigilantly on guard and alert to the signs of what's real and what's not, what's rational and irrational, is extremely important in today's society. This promotes connection and a feeling of control.

Finally, the project was finished. Just in time for the party! They were all amazed at how *real* they looked. Brighten exclaimed, "Wow, success! It looks like we are really there singing those songs. It is sort of eerie. It's a good thing we have each other to reinforce what is real and what isn't. We better run and get this to our friends quickly before the party begins!" Bow howled in agreement.

They quickly got into their dune buggy with all the equipment for the hologram and dropped it off at the Old Neighborhood Community Center, where the party would be. Relieved, they speedily drove home to attend the block party. Suddenly, Brighten's stomach felt funny. "I think my social anxiety is acting up, Beacon," she said. "I want to go to the block party, but I'm so nervous I feel sick to my stomach."

Beacon took a moment to think and told Brighten the four questions to ask herself when feeling overwhelmed or anxious to help reduce her nervousness. First, he told her the importance of getting grounded and practicing imagery. He suggested first taking a step back and taking deep, even breaths to get grounded, then envisioning herself inside a protective bubble. The bubble protects her from the negatives in the environment while letting the positives get close. Below are the four questions:

1. What do I want to do? (My end result)
2. What part of this issue can I control?
3. Is this hurting anyone?
4. What kind of protective bubble do I need around me? Large, small, thick, thin, flexible?

Brighten thought out loud, "I want to go to the block party and make new friends. I can control who I go with, how I get there, who I talk to or don't, what I consume, my personal movements, the time I arrive and the time I leave, my thoughts, and my breathing. It's not hurting anyone except me if I don't go. So, I'm envisioning a protective bubble around me to prevent people from stepping on my toes. Therefore, I avoid getting hurt."

All three arrived at the party eager to have an electrifying time and mingle. Brighten felt safe inside her imaginary bubble, Bow by her side and Beacon leading the way. All three were having so much fun as they looked at each other, patting each other on the back for successfully being at two places at once.

They walked up to a group of people who were laughing and seemed to be having a lot of fun. They found out their names were Bryce, Blakely, and Barrett. Three new friends for all three of them. They all connected with funny stories of past vacations and things they liked to do. They laughed together as they found commonality, feeling comfortable with each other,

giving them all a sense of control. They committed to meeting again in the future for some more fun and laughs.

Beacon looked at Bow and Brighten with a smile and said, "It looks like people can be two places at once these days." They all laughed, knowing the pros and cons of living in all these worlds.

Brighten shouted, "This day was awesome! It was filled with healthy excitement, enjoyment, and fun!"

Bow barked in agreement as they all piled into their new dune buggy and headed home.

As Beacon, Brighten, and Bow drove off, they could see the rainbow after the storm, and were thinking of the pot of gold at the other side.

CHAPTER 5
Story Analysis

Chapter 4 is repeated below and analyzed. The explanation of how **Bempathy** works is written in italics beneath each paragraph.

Handling Dilemmas and Conflicts

(Above is Chapter 4's title, which tells the theme of the story. This fun adventure has the characters working through predicaments that may motivate them to either overcome the challenge or put them in threat mode. The latter may cause negative feelings and behaviors, such as tunnel vision, focusing only on themselves, anxiety, sadness, anger, or stress. This negativity, if prolonged, can be hazardous to their mental and physical health. This story shows how to cope positively with conflicts and dilemmas.)

Beacon, Brighten, and Bow moved from their medium-sized house and medium-sized neighborhood to a bigger, brighter house and neighborhood. Even though Brighten was excited and happy about her new move to a better place, she also felt a loss and a fear of missing out, FOMO.

Leaving all her friends and her old neighborhood frightened Brighten. She had bouts of loneliness and a feeling of disconnection. She tended to stay in her room and engaged only digitally with her friends. Sometimes her friends were slow to respond, causing her to get upset and anxious. Bow sensed this and nuzzled up to her often to try to decrease her anxiety and sadness.

*(The above paragraphs illustrate **Dynamic Watchfulness** in that Bow was Brighten's accomplice, helping her to see she is not alone in this world and that there are different perspectives. **Empathy, communication, connectedness,** and **comfortability** were exhibited by Bow silently sensing her feelings and nuzzling up to her, connecting to comfort her. Bow supported her emotionally and physically, creating comfortability for Brighten.)*

Beacon, on the other hand, enjoys new environments, finding them exciting. He keeps up with his friends by texting or calling them to get together and do fun things. As Beacon, Brighten, and Bow were unpacking all their belongings,

Brighten began ruminating and she started to cry. Bow, her faithful dog who helped her make sense of things, stayed by her side, snuggling up to her for a hug. Brighten loved having Bow around for comfort because Bow always understood her.

*(The above paragraph illustrates **communication, commonality, comfortability**, and banter with empathy, which is **Bempathy**. Beacon kept in contact with his old friends, communicating, bantering, and finding comfortability by doing fun things together. Also Brighten felt "understood" and comforted by Bow with a hug.)*

Beacon looked perplexed and said, "Brighten, what's wrong?"

Brighten was saddened and said, "I'm upset about my old friends forgetting me, and afraid that no one in the new neighborhood will like me."

Beacon reflected on what Brighten said. He then consoled his sister with one of the many analogies he liked to use when problems arose. "Think of life as mathematical equations," he said. "Let's do a math lesson!"

*(The above paragraphs illustrate **communication** and banter with empathy, which is **Bempathy**. In asking "What's wrong?" and then consoling her, Beacon heard and understood Brighten's sadness.)*

Brighten sighed and slumped simultaneously in exasperation because she didn't like math.

Beacon quickly went to his whiteboard, which they keep accessible because they know writing things down helps people make sense of things, keep track, and feel more in control. Beacon said, "Let's look at pluses and minuses. Brighten, if I gave you $100 and added $100 more, what would you get?"

She laughed, "That's easy, $200!"

Beacon smiled and proceeded to do more. "Now let's change that sign to a minus. What is the total now?"

Brighten frowned and said, "A big fat zero."

*(The above paragraphs illustrate **communication, connectedness, control,** and **Bempathy**. Beacon used the whiteboard to demonstrate involving more senses to improve communication. Brighten laughing and shouting out answers illustrated her connecting and feeling more in control of the situation. **Dynamic Watchfulness** was displayed by Beacon being Brighten's accomplice, offering another perspective.)*

Beacon suggested, "That's what happens in life when we have too many negatives. If you keep subtracting throughout the day with negative thoughts and/or actions, you will have a big fat zero at the end of the day. There are only twenty-four hours in the day, so replace the negatives with positives or turn the negatives into positives, making life run smoother."

He suggested, "How about we try the Map of Reflection game? This will help you put things in perspective, prioritize what is beneficial in your life, and remove unwanted negatives. So, when doing your Map of Reflection, you need to ask yourself if the things in your life are adding or subtracting. Then choose where you want to place them in relation to yourself in the center. You are the most important person in your world; therefore, you are located in the center of your Map of Reflection and all the people, places, and things in your life surround you."

Bow wagged her tail in excitement, barking at this new, groundbreaking way to gain more control over their lives.

Brighten looked confused and said, "I don't want to be self-centered!"

*(The above paragraphs illustrate **communication**. Beacon was explaining a concept to Brighten. Bow was finding **connectedness** exhibited by her wagging tail, whereas Brighten was working toward connectedness.)*

Beacon laughed. "This doesn't mean you are self-centered. You are the center of *your* world, not the center of *the* world. When we put ourselves first, that means we are conscious of ourselves and how our feelings and behavior affect our world and vice versa. You are giving yourself unconditional love. Our time and attention are limited, which makes every minute valuable. Since we don't have control over our forever-changing world, what do we have control over?"

Brighten shouted, "Our time and attention and what we do with it!"

Bow howled, jumping up and down in excitement.

*(The above paragraphs illustrate **communication, commonality, connectedness, comfortability, control, commitment**, and **Bempathy**. Beacon showed empathy by smiling and explaining. Brighten and Bow jumping up and down and shouting out the answer showed finding commonality, connecting, feeling more comfortable and in control of the situation, ready to commit to the next step. They all bantered with empathy. **Dynamic Watchfulness** was exhibited by Beacon being Brighten's accomplice, showing her a different way to look at her current situation.)*

Beacon smiled as he drew a picture of the Map of Reflection. He began lecturing, as he liked to do. "Making a list of the people, places, and things in your life, then placing them in the specific rings will organize your desires, needs, and wants. You can visually see your placements. Pay close attention to those things you might think are necessary, but, *upon reflection*, can be released into the 'Spring Cleaning' section. Just because something is in Spring Cleaning doesn't mean that it can't fluctuate back into a closer part of your life later. This might include old friends; old feelings, like resentment; or places, like work and school."

Beacon went on. "Think of your Map of Reflection as your world displayed flat, and you are in the center reacting to your world as your world reacts to you. The blue section is the water around, it ebbs and flows. The things in that area are floating, and they may fall off your world or swim back into your life when and if *you* decide. This is your reflection of your present world."

Stepping away from the board, Beacon said, "Consider all areas of your life: family, faith/spiritual, social, occupation, leisure activities, psychological and emotional distractions, personal development, and vanity-related priorities. Be honest with yourself. This is your Map of Reflection in a snapshot of time, open to change as often as necessary. After you complete your Map of Reflection, sometimes doing the Conversing with Self, it will help clarify your reflection even more. All of this is a part of Dynamic Watchfulness."

*(The above paragraphs illustrate **communication** along with **Bempathy**. Beacon showed empathy by smiling as he communicates his game to Brighten and Bow.)*

Brighten then made a list of three categories—persons, places, and things—and wrote down everything in her life. She placed the information into the different rings in the drawing of her Map of Reflection. She prioritized without thinking of boundaries because boundaries get too complicated. Boundaries put limits on a person's life, which is why the Map of Reflection works better. It regulates your intimate relationships between people, places, and things.

*(The above paragraph illustrates **communication, empathy, connecting** and **commonality**. Brighten empathized, connecting with Beacon by what Beacon suggested, the Map of Reflection, and finding commonality.)*

Brighten shared her insights after doing the Map of Reflection game. "Wow, after visually reflecting, I can see old friends are still in my life, and new friends are on the horizon," she said. "This game got me to ask myself, 'How come I allow persons, places, and things to control my mood, thoughts, and behavior? Am I really upset with someone or something else, or actually upset with myself?' I am the center of my world; therefore, I can choose how I respond. Everything I do or is done to me is 'noise,' like the static on the phone or glitches when Zooming. This frustrates me, causing things to be harder to see and understand. This map helps me filter out some of my noise so I can hear myself think and hear others more clearly."

*(The above paragraph illustrates **communication, commonality, connectedness, comfortability, control, commitment,** and **Bempathy**. Brighten talked to herself, empathizing, and using all six key elements. She realized she has more control in life than she thought.)*

Just as Brighten finished her statement, Bow saw a squirrel and chased it, barking all the way to their neighbor's house. Brighten ran after her, bumping into a new young neighbor who stopped Bow by grabbing her collar. Brighten felt awkward and embarrassed about Bow not being on a leash. She didn't know what to say except "thank you" and ran back home with Bow.

*(The above paragraph illustrates **communication** and banter with empathy, which is **Bempathy**. Brighten, Bow, and the Neighbor communicated utilizing Bempathy, both behaviorally and verbally. This was illustrated by Bow running, Brighten saying thank you, and the neighbor grabbing the collar.)*

Brighten bowed her head. "Beacon, I just don't know what to do with myself," she said. "The only place I feel comfortable and safe is in my room! My mind tells me to go out and have fun with our neighbors, but my anxiety tells me 'NO' which stops me. I'm just not motivated."

Bow nudged Brighten toward the door, barking, wanting her to go visit the neighbor.

*(The above paragraphs illustrate **communication** and **Bempathy**. Brighten communicated her feelings and thoughts while Bow empathized, nudging Brighten towards the neighbor.)*

Brighten shook her head in frustration over how her thoughts didn't match her behavior and sighed. She felt conflicted. Just then, she had an epiphany.

This is a great time to say my affirmations, Brighten thought. *When I did the game Conversing with Self, I found out saying affirmations are baby steps toward reaching my goals. What affirmations should I think and say?* She continued in deep thought. *I know!*

Just then, Brighten started to repeat a realistic affirmation. She knew she liked some people, and some people liked her, so she dropped the word "some" and said, "I like people and people like me!" Brighten immediately started to smile.

Beacon asked her, "What are you thinking?"

She smiled and said, "Positive thoughts! Let's put our heads together to come up with a solution about our friend situation!"

*(The above paragraphs illustrate **communication** and **Bempathy**. Here, Brighten was communicating, empathizing with herself, illustrated by asking herself questions silently.)*

The trio sat together thinking about what to do about their friends. They thought and thought and thought about what to do with this dilemma. Conversing back and forth, trying to come up with a solution, led to them all getting headaches. They decided to take a break from the issue and relax by playing fetch with Bow.

*(The above paragraph illustrates **communication** and **Bempathy**. All three characters were communicating by bantering, giving suggestions, then stepping back from the issue to relax and take a break from the situation to see the bigger picture more clearly.)*

Bow was having so much fun fetching. She was on a roll. She saw the mail carrier and started to chase them down the street.

Beacon and Brighten immediately ran after her, screaming all the way, "STOP!"

It's a good thing that Bow loves everyone and can see all different perspectives. She happily wagged her tail and opened her mouth so the mail carrier could put the mail there. Bow, being a compromiser, decided that the pile of mail needed to be distributed fairly, and dropped it on the floor for all to share and sort by name.

*(The above paragraphs illustrate **communication, connectedness, commonality, commitment, Dynamic Watchfulness,** and **Bempathy**. Communication is illustrated by all three characters going from working together playing fetch to splitting up and running after Bow. Beacon and Brighten found commonality in wanting to catch Bow, getting them connected and committed to running after her and catching her. Bow showed how to compromise by letting Beacon and Brighten pick out their own mail by name instead of keeping all the mail herself and chewing it up. Dynamic Watchfulness was exhibited with them all being an accomplice for each other by supporting each other's actions.)*

Beacon and Brighten saw letters with their names on them and opened them up. To Brighten's surprise, she had received an invitation from her old friends, requesting that both she and her brother come to a birthday party! The invitations also asked them to sing duets, which is what they usually did at parties. They were known for their fabulous voices and creating witty songs. Together they said, "Wow, this is fantastic!" They all jumped up and down with joy and excitement.

*(The above paragraph illustrates **communication, compromising, commonality, connecting, comfortability, control,** and **Bempathy.** As Beacon and Brighten bantered, they exhibited empathy by compromising, sharing the mail and only taking their own envelopes. They all found commonality, making them feel more connected, therefore increasing comfortability with each other, making them feel more in control of themselves and the situation. This was displayed when together they all said, "Wow, this is fantastic!")*

As Brighten opened a second letter, her facial expression went from happy to befuddlement. Beacon asked, "What's wrong, Brighten? You look troubled."

Brighten frowned. "We have a dilemma," she said. "We are both invited to two important parties at once: one with our old friends, and one with our new ones. Now I have a chance to meet new friends at this block party, but I also want to keep in touch with my old friends. I don't know what to do!"

*(The above paragraphs illustrate **communication, commonality, connectedness,** and **Bempathy.** They communicated empathy by bantering (Bempathizing), as illustrated both verbally and behaviorally. This was displayed when Beacon saw Brighten's frown and questioned, "What's wrong, Brighten? You look troubled?" Through this dilemma, they found commonality because they both were involved, which made them feel more connected to the situation.)*

Beacon looked at the invitation from their old friends and smiled. "Brighten, what our old friends really want is for us to sing our duets and be the entertainment for the party," he said. "I understand you don't want to disappoint your friends and you would like to go to both events, but you physically cannot."

Brighten frowned and said, "You're right, as usual."

*(The above paragraphs illustrate **communication, commonality, connectedness, comfortability, control, commitment, Dynamic Watchfulness,** and **Bempathy.** Beacon and Brighten communicated empathy by bantering (Bempathizing), as illustrated both verbally and behaviorally. Their actions matched*

their facial expressions, as displayed by Beacon smiling after coming up with an answer and Brighten frowning, feeling distraught over the conflict of not being able to be in two places at once. Dynamic Watchfulness was exhibited by Beacon showing Brighten a different perspective.)

Beacon pondered briefly and said, "Let's step back and think of some possibilities. When we did our duets in front of our friends, how did they respond?"

Brighten's eyes widened. "They roared for more and some of them actually recorded what we sang on their phones," she said.

Beacon asked, "Do you think all our old friends will bring their phones to the party?"

Brighten laughed and said, "They don't leave their homes without them."

*(The above paragraphs illustrate **communication, commonality, connectedness, comfortability, Dynamic Watchfulness,** and **Bempathy.** Dynamic Watchfulness was exhibited by Beacon saying, "Let's step back and think of some possibilities." They both found commonality, which increased their connectedness between each other, getting them to feel more comfortable with the dilemma, as illustrated by Brighten laughing.)*

Beacon held up a finger, which was a common habit when he thought an idea had merit. "What would you say to making a holographic display of us singing duets and then sending them to our old friends?" he asked.

Brighten chuckled and responded, "Fantabulous! You saved the day! Now I won't feel guilty about going to the block party to meet new friends the same day." All three jumped up and down, laughing in unison.

*(The above paragraphs illustrate **communication, commonality, connectedness, comfortability, control, commitment,** and **Dynamic Watchfulness.** The characters communicated commonality, getting them to connect as shown by Brighten saying "Fantabulous!" in agreement. This led them both to feel more comfortable with the situation, giving a sense of control and getting them to commit to doing a project together. They displayed Dynamic Watchfulness by seeing another perspective.)*

Brighten and Bow's faces beamed. Bow cocked her head, gave a canine smile, and wagged her tail at the thought of doing this. Beacon suggested, "All we need is some reasonable equipment, hologram film, virtual reality glasses, and a projector to do a 3D scan of us singing together. Then we just animate the scan. What a fun project!"

Brighten giggled and said, "Wow, what an enlightening idea, Beacon! We will be 'unreal'—bigger than life! Our friends love holograms and virtual reality because it is exciting and entertaining. This will get them to associate us with being fun and amazing!"

*(The above paragraphs illustrate **communication, commonality, connectedness, comfortability, control, commitment, Dynamic Watchfulness,** and **Bempathy.** The characters communicated, bantering with empathy by finding commonality, and thereby connecting, demonstrated by Brighten and Bow's faces beaming and Brighten saying that Beacon's idea was "enlightening." Brighten adding to Beacon's suggestion displayed comfortability; she felt more in control of the situation and wanted to commit to this project. Seeing another perspective and adding to it illustrates Dynamic Watchfulness.)*

All three got together planning on how to accomplish this feat. They spent hours researching on All three got together to plan how they would accomplish this feat. They spent hours researching on the internet, talking, and writing down what to do for their hologram presentation. Each one was given different duties. Beacon was in charge of working with the laser, cutting, and setting up for the 3D hologram. Brighten was in charge of working with the animation portion and Bow, as usual, was there to oversee everything and make sure it was done right.

*(The above paragraph illustrates **communication, commonality, connectedness, comfortability, control, commitment, Dynamic Watchfulness,** and **Bempathy.** Dynamic Watchfulness is displayed by each character communicating about what role they are playing in the project and being able to compromise on who does what. The characters found commonality doing the same project and increasing connection with each other. This got them to feel more comfortable, increasing their feeling of control over the dilemma and strengthening their commitment to finishing the project.)*

As they progressed, they talked about the importance of using Dynamic Watchfulness as they created a hologram that was a "fake" version of themselves. They asked each other how this would affect their relationships. They agreed it would be both positive and negative. The positive is that this was fun and both sides will win. The negative is that we have one brain and so far, we cannot be split in half to experience being in two places at once. So, we will miss the fun that our friends experience watching us. This is a part of being dynamic in their watchfulness.

*(The above paragraph illustrates **communication, commonality, connectedness, comfortability, control, Dynamic Watchfulness,** and **Bempathy.** The characters exhibit Dynamic Watchfulness throughout the paragraph. They were all each other's accomplice, opening their eyes to what is real and what is not. They realized the effects this distinction has on each of them. Examining the pros and cons of a situation illustrated bantering with empathy. This atmosphere of questioning oneself and each other created commonality, increasing connectedness and making them all feel more comfortable. This gave a sense of control and helped our characters want to commit to each other during this time.)*

Beacon commented how wonderful it was to have trusting individuals in his life, like Brighten and Bow. "Making one true friend in the real world can help give us another perspective," he said. "This is a large part of what distinguishes Dynamic Watchfulness from mindfulness."

Brighten and Bow smiled in agreement as they looked forward to finishing their project.

*(The above paragraphs illustrate **communication, commonality, connectedness, comfortability, control, commitment,** and **Dynamic Watchfulness.** We can see Dynamic Watchfulness in action throughout the paragraphs. They communicated commonality, increasing their connection with each other which increased their comfort, making them feel more in control and committed. This is seen when Brighten and Bow smiled in agreement.)*

Beacon and Brighten realized that when our brain is immersed in virtual reality, it gets confused, thinking it is real. Having another person to help us practice caution by being vigilantly on guard and alert to the signs of what's real and what's not, what's rational and irrational, is extremely important in today's society. This promotes connection and a feeling of control.

*(The above paragraph illustrates a narrative explaining the importance of **Dynamic Watchfulness**.)*

Finally, the project was finished. Just in time for the party! They all were amazed at how *real* they looked. Brighten exclaimed, "Wow, success! It looks like we are really there singing those songs. It is sort of eerie. It's a good thing we have each other to reinforce what is real and what isn't. We better run and get this to our friends quickly before the party begins!" Bow howled in agreement.

*(The above paragraph illustrates **communication, commonality, connectedness, control, commitment**, and **Dynamic Watchfulness**. Dynamic Watchfulness was shown when Brighten said, "It's a good thing we have each other to reinforce what is real and what isn't." They bantered with empathy, communicating commonality by being amazed at the realness of the hologram, increasing a feeling of connection. Brighten felt comfortable and in control, saying they had better run and get everything over to their friends. She was committed to finishing and moving on, and Bow empathized by howling in agreement.)*

They quickly got into their dune buggy with all the equipment for the hologram and dropped it off at the Old Neighborhood Community Center, where the party would be. Relieved, they speedily drove home to attend the block party. Suddenly, Brighten's stomach felt funny. "I think my social anxiety is acting up, Beacon," she said. "I want to go to the block party, but I'm so nervous I feel sick to my stomach."

(The above paragraph describes unresolved conflict within Brighten, demonstrated by her wanting to go to the party but having anxiety that might prevent her from going.)

Beacon took a moment to think and told Brighten the four questions to ask herself when feeling overwhelmed or anxious to help reduce her nervousness. First, he told her the importance of getting grounded and practicing imagery. He suggested first taking a step back and taking deep, even breaths to get grounded, then envisioning herself inside a protective bubble. The bubble protects her from the negatives in the environment while letting the positives get close. Below are the four questions:

1. What do I want to do? (My end result)
2. What part of this issue can I control?
3. Is this hurting anyone?
4. What kind of protective bubble do I need around me? Large, small, thick, thin, flexible?

Brighten thought out loud, "I want to go to the block party and make new friends. I can control who I go with, how I get there, who I talk to or don't, what I consume, my personal movements, the time I arrive and the time I leave, my thoughts, and my breathing. It's not hurting anyone except me if I don't go. So, I'm envisioning a protective bubble around me to prevent people from stepping on my toes. Therefore, I avoid getting hurt."

*(The above three paragraphs illustrate a technique that helps give a person a sense of **control** and **connectedness** by getting them to be able to calm down during a conflict within themselves. They learn to find ways to feel comfortable in their own skin, creating the ability to fit in instead of running away from situations.)*

All three arrived at the party eager to have an electrifying time and mingle. Brighten felt safe inside her imaginary bubble, Bow by her side and Beacon leading the way. All three were having so much fun as they looked at each other, patting each other on the back for successfully being at two places at once.

*(The above paragraph illustrates **communication** and empathizing, displayed by the three of them having an electrifying time and patting each other on the back.)*

They walked up to a group of people who were laughing and seemed to be having a lot of fun. They found out their names were Bryce, Blakely, and Barrett. Three new friends for all three of them. They all connected with funny stories of past vacations and things they liked to do. They laughed together as they found commonality, feeling comfortable with each other, giving them all a sense of control. They committed to meeting again in the future for some more fun and laughs.

*(The above paragraph illustrates **communication, commonality, connectedness, comfortability, control,** and **commitment.** The characters communicated banter with empathy, finding commonality, and connecting with each other to increase their comfort and control. As a result, they committed to seeing each other again. The characters were depicted laughing, telling stories, and making new friends.)*

Beacon looked at Bow and Brighten with a smile and said, "It looks like people can be two places at once these days." They all laughed, knowing the pros and cons of living in all these worlds.

Brighten shouted, "This day was awesome! It was filled with healthy excitement, enjoyment, and fun!"

Bow barked in agreement as they all piled into their new dune buggy and headed home.

As Beacon, Brighten, and Bow drove off, they could see the rainbow after the storm, and were thinking of the pot of gold at the other side.

*(The above paragraphs illustrate **communication, commonality, connectedness, comfortability, control, commitment, Dynamic Watchfulness,** and **Bempathy.** Dynamic Watchfulness was demonstrated when they acknowledged there are pros and cons to all the worlds in which we live, and we need to be aware of how to balance them. The characters all connected, finding commonality, which increased their ability to feel comfortable and feel in control of their current situation. They committed to moving forward, as displayed by them driving off in their dune buggy.)*

*(All of the chapters illustrate **communication** utilizing **Bempathy.**)*

CHAPTER 6
Conclusion: Putting It All Together

While reading this book, with which character did you identify the most? Beacon the leader, Brighten the follower, Bow the compromiser, or all of them?

When reading, were you thinking about the six key elements in Bempathy? Did you find any of the six elements described below?

1. Communication — The ability to send and receive information that another person will understand; the ability to send and receive information to oneself.
2. Commonality — Two or more people who share the same or similar characteristics, interests, or experiences on such subjects as people, places, or things.
3. Connectedness — A feeling of fitting in or being linked with self or one or more people.
4. Comfortability — The ability to feel comfortable in a situation and/or with self; feeling physically and/or emotionally at ease; freedom from emotional or physical pain.
5. Control — The ability to perceive power, exercise limits, or have a guiding influence over situations and self.
6. Commitment — The state of being dedicated or loyal to self, something, or someone.

Were you thinking about how the characters exhibited Dynamic Watchfulness, which is defined below?

1. The state of being active and present in the multiple worlds—reality, virtual reality, metaverse, internet, inner self, and others that are constantly evolving—that constitute our lives, and understanding the difference between them.
2. The quality or state of being aware of and attentive to the consequences of actions in the context of multiple information sources, such as reality, virtual reality, metaverse, internet, inner self, and cybernetics.
3. Continuous observation of oneself, electronic devices, and others; understanding what is done or occurs; practicing caution, discretion, and self-restraint; being vigilantly on guard and alert to

4. Happiness 3. Fear 2. Disgust

6. Surprise 5. Sadness 1. Anger

3. Fear 4. Happiness 6. Surprise

1. Anger 2. Disgust 5. Sadness

signs; watchfully anticipating and maintaining respect for all worlds.
4. The use of the five senses, as well as help from others, to be dynamic in our watchfulness of all the worlds in which we live.

The answers for Page 14 are on the previous page, showing what faces match the emotions.

Directions for how to do the Map of Reflection:

1. Make three different lists titled Persons, Places, and Things. Under each category, list all that is in your life at this moment. Even if you don't physically have it, it may be lingering emotionally or cognitively in your mind. This would go under the "Things" list. For example, a lost job, emotional baggage like resentment or anger, or a desire to go on vacation.
2. Put an X by the people, places, and things that are negative and take away from your life.
3. Anything that has an X by it gets moved into the blue section (Spring Cleaning).
4. In each category, circle the people, places, and things that are positive and add to your life.
5. Place the circled ones in the rings that you believe correspond with their position in your life: green, orange, or gold.
6. To determine what to place inside the ring closest to you (orange: things you would die without), please see page 11, Broken Heart Syndrome.
7. Ask yourself, who or what do I want coming with me on my journey at this time?
8. The "Things" section is everything left over in your world after you complete people and places.

Definitions of Persons, Places and Things:

Consider all areas of your life: personal, professional, social, psychological, spiritual, emotional, and behavioral.

Persons: Other people in your life directly or indirectly, such as family, friends, co-workers, peers, medical personnel, etc.

Places: Physical environment or surroundings, any place you frequent, real or virtual. It could include the house, office, etc. and also the internet.

Things: Pets, leisure, hobbies, self-care, and emotional or behavioral baggage, in addition to other stuff you have.

Benefits of Map of Reflection:

- Offers reminders of what works and what doesn't
- Keeps things in perspective
- Helps prioritize
  - What do you really need, and what is unnecessary?
- Helps you visually see what is important
- Aids with organization
- Helps you create balance in your life
- Gives direction
- Uses categorization to help you see what you can survive without
- Allows you to add more content by regularly spring cleaning
- Offers a chance for introspection about people and relationships
  - Are these people unreliable, critical, competitive, or irritating?
  - What kind of people do you want in your life?
- Aligns priorities
- Inspires you to get unstuck, move forward
- Helps you break away from things that hold you back
- Requires you to visually see hard-to-face truths about unhealthy aspects of your life
- Highlights that action creates a reaction (you react to your environment; the environment reacts to you)
- Decreases stress by removing physical and emotional clutter
- Offers a place to start if you are overwhelmed
- Decreases noise and static in our lives
- Acknowledges that reflection is ever-changing, cycling, and fluctuating
- Can start from outside-in or inside-out, whichever is comfortable

- Identifies who is an asset rather than a liability
- Makes transitions manageable

Bempathy creates positive reciprocal relationships by using the six key elements while being dynamically watchful. Since we are the center of our world, our world reacts to us, and we react to it. When **communicating** with people, places, and things in our many worlds, it is important to find **commonality**, thereby increasing **connectedness**. This gets us to feel more **comfortable** in the situation, which increases a sense of **control** and produces a **commitment** to move from point A to point B.

Conflict in our lives is inevitable, whether situational or within ourselves. Beacon, Brighten, and Bow's story illustrates how to resolve issues in a positive way using **Bempathy**. It's not the conflict that is negative; it is how people deal with it that can be negative. Using the **Bempathy** way will help you and others to make most situations win/win by creating "positive conflict."

Positive conflict fosters:
- New ideas
- Creativity
- Problem-solving
- Flexibility
- An ability to listen and really hear what others are saying
- Solutions
- Communication skills
- Setting appropriate limits
- Emotional control
- Opportunities to verbalize your needs
- Balancing power positions

Let's work with conflicts instead of running from them. If the conflict turns into a dilemma where neither solution is the best, this is a good time to make your choice either by stepping back or using your accomplice. Remember nothing is absolute, so there will be some conflicts that we may need to step away from.

This book helps people find "knowledge by observing objectively with mind & body & internet to connect with you all" which forms the acronym KOOMBIYA.

Ask yourself, are you a leader, a follower, or a compromiser? In this particular conflict, do you need a leader, a compromiser, or a follower to move forward? These are important things to think about if your conflict turns into a dilemma.

Are you dedicated to gaining healthy excitement and new relationships, while keeping the old ones? If so, you are committed. Remember, on your journey, everyone is different and has their own language style. No one is perfect. What a relief! Be your authentic self like Beacon, Brighten, and Bow and bravely enjoy your life adventures using **Bempathy**. Once we leave the safety of the screen and our digital devices, it can be awkward and scary. Other people are also trying to find out who they are and feeling vulnerable at times, just like you.

Using Bempathy will help create reciprocal communication, producing balance and compromise in your life and others. Most importantly, remember: Life is perception and perception is life!

Beacon leads the way, Brighten follows and is enlightened, and Bow helps connect the dots. Which one are you? Are you all of them put together? Which delightful character best fits you?

Beacon, Brighten, and Bow are looking forward to seeing you again on their next escapade describing more fun ways to Bempathize.

References

American Psychological Association. (2021). *U.S. Adults Report Highest Stress Level Since Early Days of the COVID-19 Pandemic* [Press Release]. https://www.apa.org/news/press/releases/2021/02/adults-stress-pandemic

American Psychological Association. (2022). *Inflation, war push stress to alarming levels at two-year COVID-19 anniversary* [Press Release]. https://www.apa.org/news/press/releases/2022/03/inflation-war-stress

Chamorro–Premuzic, T. (2014, May 13). How the web distorts reality and impairs our judgement skills. *The Guardian.* https://www.theguardian.com/media-network/media-network-blog/2014/may/13/internet-confirmation-bias

Cleveland Clinic. (2020, February 12). Can You Die of a Broken Heart? — And Other Emotional Questions. *Health Essentials.* https://health.clevelandclinic.org/can-die-broken-heart-emotional

Healthwise Staff. (2022, April 29). Learning About Broken Heart Syndrome. *MyHealth.Alberta.ca.* https://myhealth.alberta.ca/Health/aftercareinformation/pages/conditions.aspx?hwid=abr6045&

Kramer, A., Guillory, J., Hancock, J. (2014, June 2). Experimental evidence of massive-scale emotional contagion through social networks. *Proceedings of the National Academy of Sciences (PNAS).* 111(24), 8788-8790. https://doi.org/10.1073/pnas.1320040111

McRaney, D. (2011, October 5). The Benjamin Franklin Effect. *You Are Not So Smart.* https://youarenotsosmart.com/2011/10/05/the-benjamin-franklin-effect

Seyfried, E. (2022, February 2). The Ben Franklin Effect. *Cape Gazette.* https://www.capegazette.com/blog-entry/ben-franklin-effect/234382

Suzuki, M & Yamamoto, Y. (2021). The Influence of Confirmation Bias on Web Search Behavior. *Frontiers in Psychology.* 12:771948. https://doi.org/10.3389/fpsyg.2021.771948

ACKNOWLEDGEMENTS

Special thanks to my husband, Byron Barnes, Jill White, and all my clients for their support and input in this book. Thanks to Taryn Lawson, Jessica Claire Haney and Ben Trittipoe for their expert editing, Cyndie Dahlberg for her book design, and to Jon Reis for his wonderful character illustrations and graphics.

My love and gratitude to my parents, brothers, and son, Taylor, who supported and encouraged me.

ABOUT THE AUTHOR

Jill Robin Payne, MA, LPC-S, LCDC, is a Licensed Professional Counselor – Supervisor and a Licensed Chemical Dependency counselor who is also Certified in Equine Assisted Psychotherapy (EAGALA).

Jill was the first student from her college to intern at the National Institutes of Health in Bethesda, Maryland. She interned at the Veterans Administration Hospital in Houston for her master's degree. While working at Bellaire Hospital in Houston she authored a guide for positive rehabilitative activities for the emotionally and physically challenged.

During her over 40 years of work experience in the mental health field, she has given numerous lectures, taught college level Behavior Modification as an adjunct professor, is an author who continues managing a diverse practice. She is heard on all social media outlets plus local and national radio and television stations commenting on the intersection of current events and social psychology.

Jill is a member of the American Counseling Association, Houston Alumnae Chapter of ZTA, Texas State Society and a lifetime member of the Houston Livestock Show and Rodeo. She holds a Bachelor of Science Degree in Recreational Therapy from Longwood University and a Master's Degree in Clinical/Counseling Psychology with honors from Houston Christian University.

Jill's practice is devoted to advancing the notion that seeking advice for mental health is as important as seeking advice for physical health. With a background in Pilates certification, reiki mastery, hypnotherapy, an undergraduate degree in recreation therapy, and a master's in psychology, she developed a concept that she copyrighted and trademarked as Bempathy® – a term she herself coined. Bempathy® represents a unique approach to communication and social skills, combining banter with empathy to build and maintain harmonious reciprocal relationships. All of Jill's work and efforts stem directly from the heart. Her passion is to 'Spread the Goodness' using the synergy of mind, body, and Bempathy®.

Jill is very versatile as a parade grand marshal and meeting a U.S. President in the Rose Garden, to being a published author and motivational speaker. Jill works to empower individuals in the choice and meaning of their relationships through lectures in seminars and symposiums at Texas Medical Center, Ultimate Women's Expo, West Houston Medical Center, The Empowered Summit, National Conference of States Societies, Embassies and Diplomatic Corporations, United Cerebral Palsy Telethon, HARCH, Rotary, and at numerous health and civic clubs in Houston and Washington, D.C. She has contracted at pain clinics and partial hospitalization programs throughout her career as a psychotherapist to facilitate stress, pain and anger management programs, and to provide cognitive behavioral therapy.

Her newly published books can be purchased on Amazon.

She resides in Houston, Texas where she maintains a private practice and lives with her husband. Her son Taylor, is doing his residency in Family Medicine.

www.jillrobinpayne.com

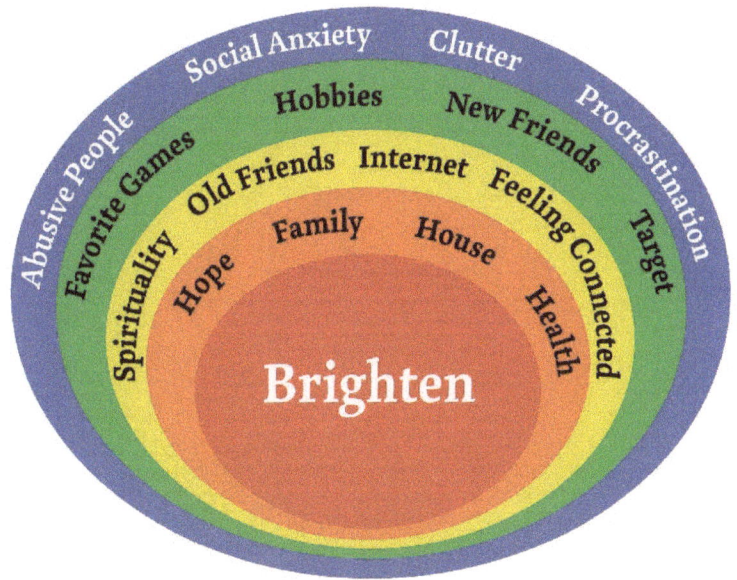

Brighten's Map of Reflection

People

(New Friends)
(Old Friends)
Abusive People
(Family)

Places

Internet
House
Target

Things

✕ Social Anxiety
✕ Clutter
✕ Procrastination
(Hobbies)
(Favorite Games)
(Spirituality)
(Hope)
(Health)
(Feeling Connected)

People   Places   Things

Your Map of Reflection

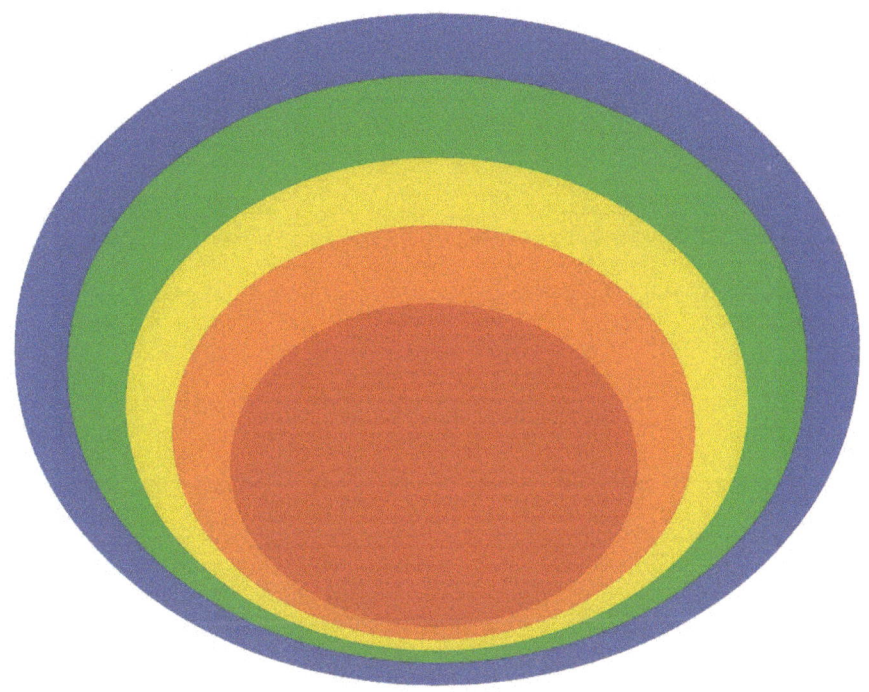

People   Places   Things

Your Map of Reflection

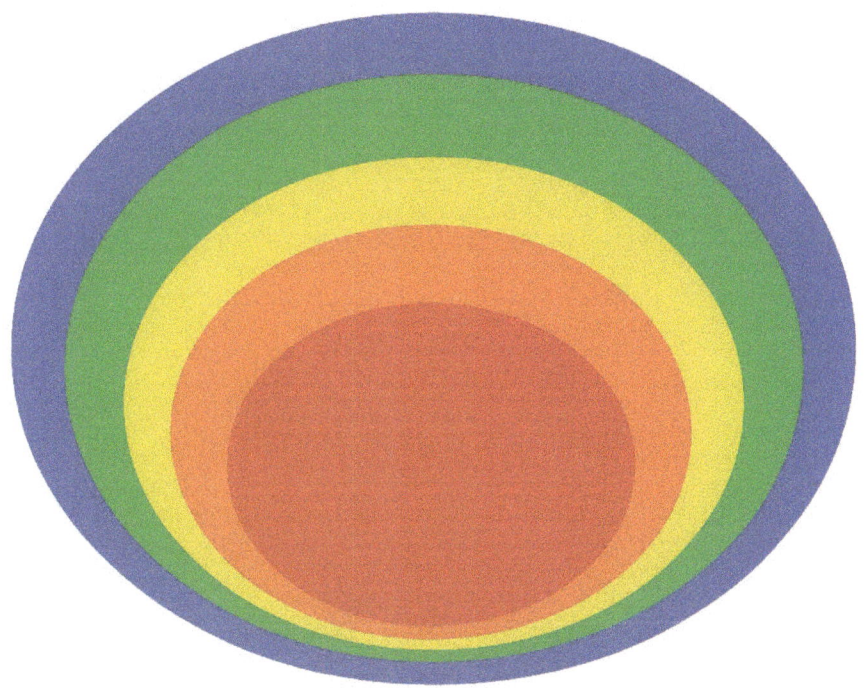

NOTES

www.ingramcontent.com/pod-product-compliance
Lightning Source LLC
Chambersburg PA
CBHW051235120626
46547CB00013B/1647